Original Title: Innermost Ink

Copyright © 2023 Book Fairy Publishing
All rights reserved.

Editors: Theodor Taimla
Autor: Annabel Swan
ISBN 978-9916-39-507-3

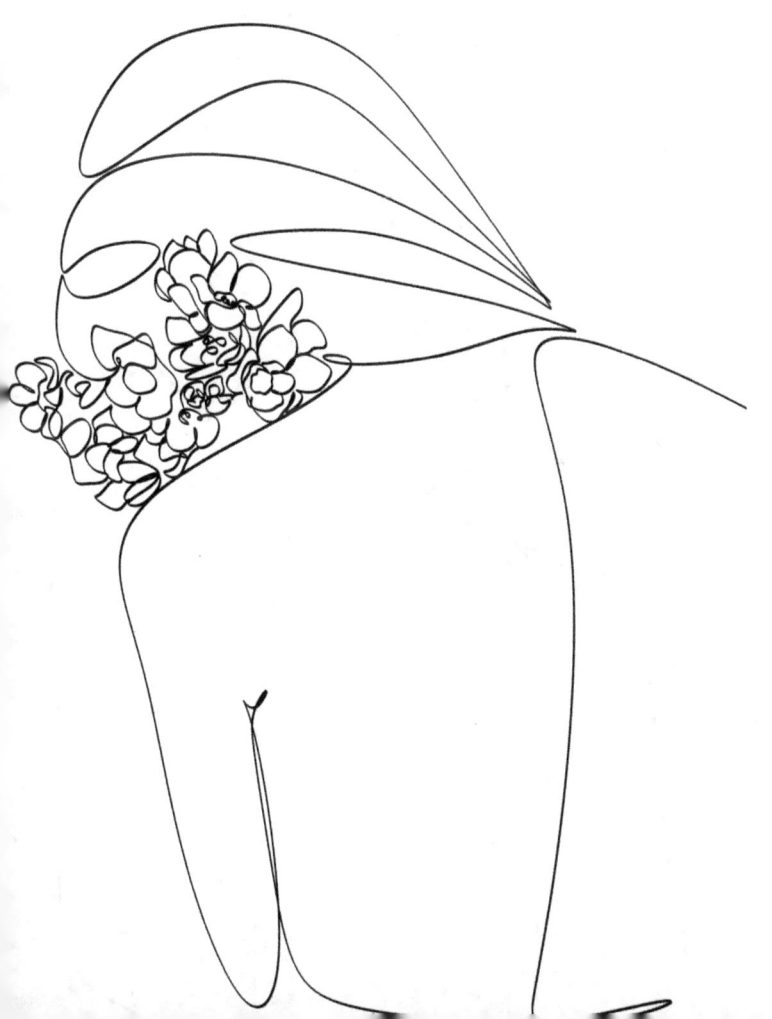

Innermost Ink

Annabel Swan

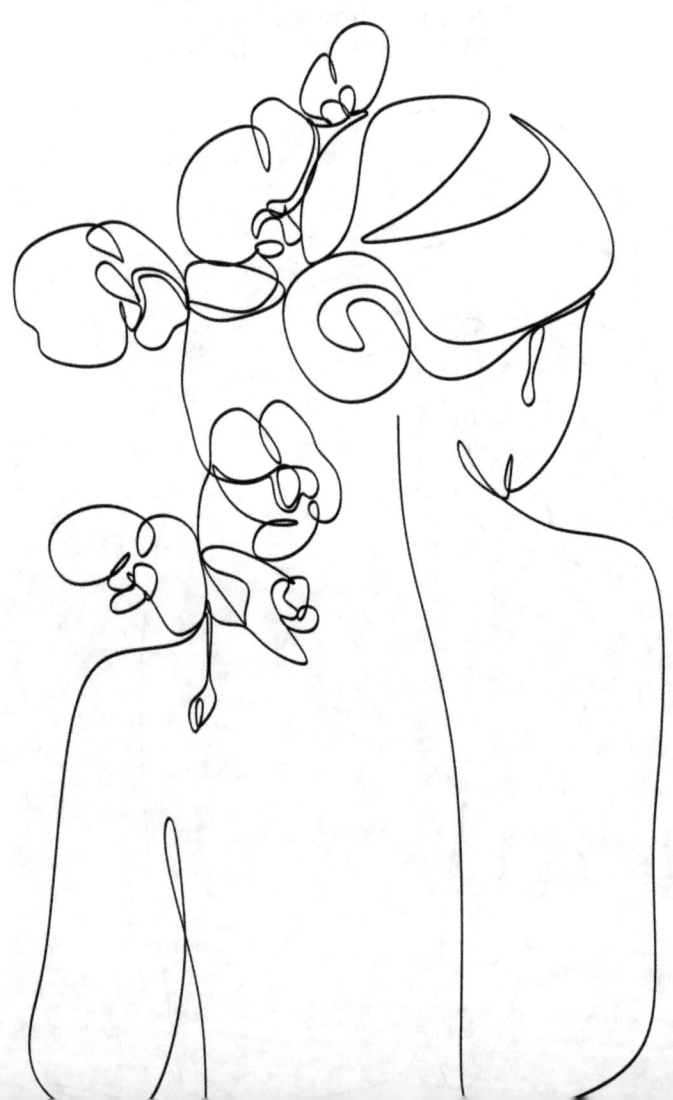

Privacy in Pigment

In strokes and hues, secrets lie,
Behind a canvas, whispers hide.
Colors cry in silent speech,
Pigments promise, solitude's beach.

Sealed in scenes none can traverse,
Every brush a private universe.
Mysteries clad in coats of art,
Privacy in pigment, a silent heart.

Hidden Haikus

Seventeen beats dance,
Unseen poems softly prance.
Words in hiding, glance.

Nature's brief story,
Captured in its quiet glory.
Silent inventory.

Moments briefly told,
In syllables brave and bold.
Haikus break the mould.

Hidden in plain sight,
Snug between day and the night.
Haikus take their flight.

Depths of Drafting

On paper plains so vast and wide,
An architect's thoughts come to reside.
Lines intersect, a calculated dance,
Drafting the depths, give dreams a chance.

Blueprints bloom, from visions sown,
In the drafter's hand, the future's hone.
Structures rise from flat confessions,
Crafted in careful, silent sessions.

Building bones with pen's caress,
In the depths of drafting, they express.
Precision weds artistic flare,
Crafting spaces with skill and care.

Woven Words

Words interlace to form a tale,
A textured tapestry, beyond the pale.
Narratives knot in a fabric spun,
Stories sewn until they are done.

Phrases fold in rhythmic pleas,
Prose that patterns like the seas.
Verses thread through every line,
In woven words, the tales entwine.

Characters caught in the weaver's loom,
Plotlines patch where fates bloom.
Imagination's cloth, endlessly unfurls,
In woven words, a world swirls.

Hushed Haikus

Silent whispers blow,
Gentle as the falling snow,
Secrets none shall know.

Moonlit shadows cast,
Figures from a quiet past,
Silhouettes that last.

Leaves in hush descend,
Calm before the night will end,
Peaceful messages send.

Streams of silence run,
Underneath the sleeping sun,
Day is almost done.

Eclipsed Emotions

In the twilight's sway,
The sun and moon cross their paths,
Emotions astray.

Feelings start to eclipse,
Lost in celestial scripts,
Heart's light slowly slips.

Shrouded love's lament,
Darkened by a heart's descent,
Seeking for ascent.

Eclipsed joy will rise,
Tears will dry from these eyes,
Hope in the skies.

Chronicles of the Core

Deep within the earth,
Furnace of a molten birth,
Origins of worth.

Tales of ancient fire,
Sculpting landscapes, steep and dire,
Natural spire.

Crafting continents,
Deep-rooted elements,
Geologic events.

The core's chronicle,
Planet's heart, so spherical,
Majestic miracle.

The Sentient Scribe

With quill in hand tight,
Scribe ignites the thoughtful night,
Words of starry light.

Ink spills on the page,
As the scribe does engage,
In wisdom of the sage.

Narratives that weave,
Stories only minds conceive,
Readers then believe.

Sentient and alive,
Through the lexicon, we dive,
The scribe's tale will thrive.

Hidden Haikus

Whispers in the breeze,
Secrets held in nature's grasp,
Haikus softly hide.

Gentle stream's murmur,
Stones cradle the water's flow,
Secret syllables.

Leaves dance to the ground,
Autumn's crisp, poetic breath,
Verses veiled in fall.

Horizon's first light,
Daybreak's haiku in pastels,
Dawn's tender haiku.

Bleeding Ballads

Notes trickle, blood-red,
Strings weep as bows tug heartstrings,
Ballads bleed in tune.

Verses pierce the night,
Melancholy in their wake,
Sonorous, they weep.

Each stanza a cut,
Rhymes carving emotions deep,
Lyric's sharp release.

Choruses cry out,
Pain in harmonious throes,
Ballads' sorrow flows.

Truths Told in Type

Inked truths march in lines,
Black and white, the page adorned,
Stories thus confined.

Typed words never blink,
Honest to the core they stay,
Courage in each clink.

Silent are the keys,
Yet their echoes shape our world,
Typing tales unfreeze.

Printed paths unwind,
Journeys through the mind's expanse,
Type reveals, entwined.

Pensive Penmanship

In each loop and line,
Thoughts entwined in cursive dance,
Penmanship defines.

Quill skims the paper,
Each word a silent whisper,
Pensive, it savors.

Mind's unvoiced discourse,
Scripted in tangled letters,
Pondering life's course.

Handwriting reveals,
In strokes and dots, the spirit,
Its cadence, it peals.

Fathomless Feelings

Beneath the surface, feelings bloom,
A silent dance in the heart's secret room.
Currents of passion, waves of despair,
In the fathomless depths, we find what's rare.

Emotions swirl in a ceaseless gyre,
Fueling within an undying fire.
Diving deep where light grows dim,
Unearthing love, a treasure grim.

In the abyss, where silence screams,
Lie buried hopes and forsaken dreams.
Fathomless feelings, in shadows cast,
Holding whispers of the vast.

Introspective Inks

With introspective inks I write,
A reflection deep of the inner fight.
The pen it glides on the silent page,
In a script it binds my hidden rage.

Thoughts process in scribbled form,
Caught in a storm that's not yet warm.
Words disclose a heart's true face,
In the inks, my soul finds grace.

Mysteries solved in mute debate,
In the strokes, my mind's estate.
Each letter a step to understand,
A quest inscribed by my own hand.

Reflections in Writing

Reflections in writing, mirrored soul,
Narratives crafted to make me whole.
On parchment plains, my spirit speaks,
Through metaphors and grammar peaks.

Life etched in ink, revealing tales,
Of victories sweet and sorrowful wails.
In every sentence, my essence caught,
A lasting echo of battles fought.

Characters rise from the depths of thought,
In dialogues of feeling fraught.
Through crafted words, I live again,
In written reflections, I remain.

Emotive Etchings

The etchings of emotive art,
Where sentiments and muses start.
The canvas bleeds in hues heartfelt,
In every stroke, my spirit's dealt.

Feelings carved on the page's skin,
Revealing paths where I've been.
The quill drips with a tender ache,
Emotions bared for my own sake.

Etchings flow from the well of pain,
As drops of joy, like summer rain.
The paper holds my heart's deep etches,
In every line, my voice fetches.

Threads of Thought

Woven on the loom of mind, stark and taut,
Intricate patterns of thinking caught.
Silken strands that twist and ply,
Holding the fabric of reason high.

Lines connect, an intricate lace,
A tapestry of contemplation's face.
Colors bleed as ideas combine,
In the quilt where thoughts intertwine.

With each weave and warp, a tale unfolds,
A story of the mind that steadily holds.
Threads of thought, thin and stout,
In the mind's loom, ever weaving out.

Mind's Mural

On the canvas of the psyche, pigments spread,
A mural of memories, alive, not dead.
Emotions brush in hues so bold,
Each stroke, a segment of story untold.

Imagination dips in palettes of dreams,
Blending the real with the fantastical it seems.
Shadows highlight the edges of thought,
Giving depth to the scenes it has wrought.

Reflections echo in colors so rife,
Painting the moments of one's life.
Mind's mural, ever shifting its view,
A gallery of the heart, forever anew.

Inner Indigo

Indigo depths, a well of the soul,
A hidden space where secrets scroll.
Darker than night, yet bright as a flame,
An inner universe, calling your name.

Dive into the depths, where whispers swim,
In the silent echo of a personal hymn.
Wisps of emotion, tinted with care,
Flow in the currents of the innermost air.

Submerge in the essence, purely you,
Where the indigo infuses every hue.
Tranquil waters of the mind's own sea,
Reflect the myriad, the true self set free.

Shadowed Sonnets

In the quiet nooks where light seldom treads,
Rest the shadowed sonnets, unsaid.
Verses veiled in the dusk of mind,
Where the deepest contours of self are confined.

Whispers of the night, draped in obscure verse,
In the silent theater of the universe.
Words move like ghosts, soft and slow,
In the dance of shadows, they ebb and flow.

Ink drips from the quill of the moon's soft glow,
Scribing sonnets where dark emotions grow.
A tender touch on parchment bereft of light,
Where thoughts convene in the solace of night.

Codex of the Heart

Whispers embedded in the silent beats,
A parchment of emotions, where pulse entreats,
Intricate scripts on a canvas so pure,
Love's dialect, silent, yet secure.

Chapters of passion inscribed within,
A tome of warmth beneath the skin,
Verses of ardor, tenderly impart,
Binding the leaves of the codex heart.

An anthology of feelings, vast and deep,
In the heart's core, where secrets keep,
Narratives of joy and sorrow's art,
Scribed in the codex of the heart.

Layers of Lexicon

Words, like veils of varied verse,
Silken, hiding truths diverse,
Each a layer, a nuanced sheath,
Cloaking subtleties that breathe.

Lexicon, a tapestry rewoven,
Meanings nested, some yet unspoken,
Plying through the fabric of speech,
In the layers, new insights reach.

Syntax and context align in tiers,
Conveying thoughts through the years,
Language's stratums, dense and complex,
In the quiet depth of lexicon's annex.

Cryptic Calligraphy

Ink traces paths, cryptic and snug,
On parchment, it dances, a mystical bug,
The scribe's hand waltzes in arcane delight,
Penning enigmas from day into night.

Eloquent loops dress secrets in swirls,
Calligraphy's mystery gracefully unfurls,
Each stroke a cipher, a hidden key,
Unlocking the vaults of secrecy.

Scripted riddles wrapped in charm,
Curling runes that disarm,
Elegant letters, cryptic dance,
In the calligraphy, we find our chance.

Manifesting Muses

Whence come these muses, in shadows attired,
To kindle the soul, so brightly inspired?
They weave the world with a dreamer's thread,
In visions painted, in whispers spread.

Plucking the strings of imagination's lyre,
Igniting thoughts with creative fire,
Muses cavort on the mind's grand stage,
Their touch converting the blank page.

Ether's children, invisible hands,
Sculpting ideas from etherial sands,
In the heart's studio, they play their roles,
Crafting wonder from the coals.

Enigma of Expression

Within the heart a mystery lies,
Words dance quietly in disguise.
Unraveled thoughts behind the eyes,
Scribe the soul's silent cries.

Echoes of emotions swell,
An enigma that lips dare not tell.
In the silence, feelings dwell,
Within expression's secret spell.

Artful whispers of the mind,
Intangible, they twist and wind.
A cryptic script of one's own kind,
Leaving common tongue behind.

In the depth of quiet glances,
Expression its own dance dances.
Every gesture, a tale it chances,
In the enigma's vast expanses.

Palette of Privacy

Hues and shades of inner space,
A canvas veiled by public face.
Colors mix in subtle grace,
Privacy—the artist's sacred place.

Brush strokes of thought gently blend,
Where boundaries of self extend.
Solitary pigments comprehend,
The palette where our secrets wend.

Concealed beneath the surface wide,
Lie layers of self that we confide.
The colors that we choose to hide,
In privacy's palette, there reside.

Within this artful, quiet shrine,
Our truest selves we refine.
In privacy's palette, we design,
The inner spectrum, purely mine.

Inner Etymology

Words stem from roots so deep,
In the mind's fertile soil they sleep.
Bursting through with a leap,
In inner etymology, meanings steep.

Ancestral echoes in speech reside,
Time's passage they effortlessly bide.
From ancient tongues, they glide,
In linguistic dance, far and wide.

From within the heart's domain,
Emotions give semantics' chain.
Phrasing pain, joy, and disdain,
Words are born and then sustain.

The saga of language none can gauge,
It grows, adapts from age to age.
Our inner etymology, a timeless stage,
Where words our stories engage.

Beyond the Blotting

Beyond the ink blots, truth soars,
On paper wings, it uproariously roars.
Between the written lines, it explores,
The realm beyond the blotting's doors.

In the stillness of the unsaid word,
A symphony of understanding stirred.
Untainted by the voices heard,
In written silence, insight conferred.

The potent space between the dots,
Holds more than textual thoughts.
Where meaning's not enclosed in spots,
The tranquil place knowledge got.

Scribed lines may fade with time,
But truth transcends the aging rhyme.
Beyond the blotting, the sublime,
In unwritten cadence, it chimes.

Scribing Shadows

In the hush of twilight's fall,
Whispers dance on ancient walls.
Scribing shadows, stretching long,
The day's last light, a fading song.

In darkness, ink spills on the page,
Quiet scribe of another age.
Every stroke, a secret shared,
The moonlit quill, a solitaire.

Ghosts of lore, in silence weave,
Tales untold, the night conceives.
Mysteries penned in silver glow,
Shadows scribe what stars bestow.

With dawn, these dusky words alight,
Vanished tales in morning's sight.
Yet in the shadows, truth prevails,
A whispered story never fails.

Quietude and Quills

In the realm of quietude,
Quills dance on pergamen.
Hallowed words in solitude,
From the silent poet's pen.

Gentle strokes on parchment worn,
In the still of a heartbeat's pause.
Beneath the wane of a crescent morn,
Each line, a whispered cause.

Through tranquil air the verses soar,
Elusive as the evening's chill.
The calm that speaks, and speaks no more,
Quietude and quills fulfill.

In this cloistered, hushed retreat,
Time's echo casts its spells.
As words and stillness gently meet,
A symphony in silence swells.

Unspoken Stanzas

Words lay dormant, unsaid, unspent,
In the heart's secretive enclave.
Unspoken stanzas, meanings meant,
Silent depths of an inner wave.

Within the eyes, a lexicon wide,
The tales that lips may never tell.
The muted verses that reside,
In the soul's echoing well.

The quiet breath of thought's reveal,
Where unvoiced poems find their form.
In unspoken stanzas, they conceal,
The silent symphony of the norm.

Yet in the hush of inner lands,
Emotions scribe with invisible hands.
In each beat, a sonnet stands,
Unspoken, yet the heart understands.

Depths of Diction

In the fathomless depths of diction,
Words plunge into vast confession.
Each phrase a timeless conviction,
A seeker's deep and devout obsession.

Beneath layers of lexicon's tide,
Meaning swirls in silent procession.
In depths of diction, truths abide,
Submerged in linguistic expression.

Here, where thoughts in words are dressed,
Language holds its sacred quest.
Within this well of the professed,
Lies the heart's unspoken zest.

So dive beneath the surface gleam,
The caverns where semantics dream.
In depths of diction, find the seam,
Where words are worlds, and worlds they teem.

The Quill's Caress

In whispered strokes, the quill does dance,
Upon the parchment in trance,
Each word a step, a tender glance,
A tale spun in delicate advance.

With inky veins, it tells its lore,
Through ages past and myths of yore,
The paper holds its weight and more,
As the quill caresses evermore.

It scripts the joy, the love, the pain,
In every droplet of its stain,
It weaves a world where dreams remain,
In the heart's silent, soft refrain.

The poet's hand, the quill's command,
Together craft a timeless land,
The script of life, by passion fanned,
Beneath the quill's gentle caress grand.

Murmurs of the Mind

Within the silent halls of thought,
The murmurs of the mind are wrought,
A secret place, with battles fought,
Where wars of whispered fears are sought.

Ideas bloom like flowers wild,
Where seeds of contemplation filed,
Each notion like a tender child,
In the embrace of musings mild.

The echoes of our inner speech,
In shadows just beyond our reach,
They form the lessons life will teach,
Within the murmurs, wisdom each.

The mind, a canvas vast and wide,
Where murmurs dance and coincide,
A symphony of thoughts that glide,
The soul's soft voice, in mind confide.

Insightful Illustrations

Each stroke of pen, each line and shade,
Insightful illustrations made,
In artful silence, thoughts parade,
Where memories and dreams cascade.

Drawn from the well of inner sight,
Where vision seeks to bring to light,
Each image tells of plight or flight,
On canvas where our truths unite.

The artist's eye, perceptive, keen,
Sees worlds that lie in veils unseen,
In colors bold or subtle sheen,
Portraying life's vast, varied scene.

From inner depths, the visions swell,
In lines where life and lore do dwell,
The tale of every stroke can tell,
Of insights in each illustration's spell.

Cryptography of the Conscious

In the mind's cryptic tapestry,
The codes and keys of 'I' and 'we',
A matrix of complexity,
Where conscious locks its deepest sea.

We cipher through our tangled thoughts,
Decrypt the lessons life has taught,
A hidden meaning, subtly wrought,
In the cryptography of our lot.

Our inner codes, at times concealed,
In layers of the self unpeeled,
Reveal the truths we've shielded, sealed,
Within the conscious mind revealed.

Thus, every heart contains a script,
In symbols blurred and oft encrypt,
In understanding, we're equipped,
To navigate the conscious crypt.

Beneath the Blots

Ink stains spread like whispers soft,
Echoes of the tales they've spun,
Secrets veiled in darkness, aloft,
A canvas where thoughts come undone.

Treasures hidden 'neath every blot,
Tales of love and battles fought,
Sorrow's veil and happiness caught,
In the silence, with meaning fraught.

Each smudge a word, a world, a thought,
On parchment, life's essence is taught,
Scribbled lines where truth is sought,
Underneath, the truths are brought.

In spaces between each inked dot,
Lies the essence that time forgot,
Speckled shadows that time begot,
Beneath the blots, our musings clot.

Soul's Script

Scripted on the soul, a hidden verse,
Engraved where life's quill begins to dance,
Secrets etched without a scribe's rehearse,
The heart's pure language, born of chance.

Each heartbeat pens a line anew,
The ink of spirit never dries,
Through joys and woes, the words accrue,
Soul's script beneath the worldly guise.

In silence, every line takes shape,
A story only felt, not seen,
Life etches deep, no chance to escape,
Narratives sown in the seams.

The soul's indelible, timeless prose,
Record of a journey through highs and lows,
Penned without pause as the life force flows,
In soul's script, the true self shows.

Submerged Sighs

Beneath the waves of waking thought,
Submerged sighs, too deep to hear,
Echoes of the battles fought,
The cost of each fallen tear.

In ocean's depth, the whispers dwell,
Unheard, unseen, but always felt,
A swell of secrets none can quell,
In liquid silence, emotions melt.

Sighs that ripple through the soul,
Sorrows drowned in fathom's keep,
Where words lose form and lose control,
And drift into the silent deep.

Beneath the still, undisturbed tides,
Are the sighs from our heart's confines,
Where the echo of truth still resides,
Submerged, yet the soul still shines.

Hues of Heartache

With every shade of somber stain,
Heartache paints in strokes of pain,
A portrait etched in silent bane,
Where sorrow's colors will remain.

In the hues of a heavy heart,
Tints of the past that won't depart,
Each memory a master's art,
A canvas torn right from the start.

Lavender twilights of regret,
Crimson tides of sunsets met,
Indigo shadows hard to forget,
A spectrum of love and the nets.

Yet in this gallery of grief,
A subtle solace finds relief,
For every hue bespeaks belief,
In heartache's hues, we find our peace.

Pensive Pigments

In hues subdued, the twilight sighs,
A canvas brushed with somber skies,
The painter's thoughts in colors blend,
Where pensive pigments softly end.

Amidst the shades of gray and blue,
The world hides secrets, old and new,
Each stroke reveals the deep unknown,
In every shade, a feeling shown.

The whispering walls of crimson red,
Tell tales of love and tears once shed,
The golden glow of morning light,
Gives hope that breaks the hold of night.

Reflections cast on mirrored lake,
As dawn's first rays the darkness break,
The vibrant life in nature's thrum,
In contemplation, thoughts become.

Resonant Reveries

In the quiet of the dreaming space,
Echoes stir, a haunting grace,
Thoughts like bells that chime so clear,
In resonant reveries, draw near.

Night's embrace holds whispers deep,
The heart's own secrets, left to keep,
Every pulse, a melody,
Sings of what was meant to be.

Stars above in chorus bright,
Hum the tunes of distant light,
Harmony in silent sound,
In the vastness, we are bound.

Sleep invites the mind to roam,
Across the seas of dreams, we comb,
A symphony of soul's desire,
In trails of stardust, hearts aspire.

Solace in Syntax

In the structure of the sentence lies,
A refuge from the world's cries,
Syntax cradles thoughts so rare,
Solace found in grammar's care.

Words weave a web of comfort tight,
Phrases dance in morning's light,
The poet's pen, the ample lexicon,
Create a bond that spans beyond.

Sentences like streams flow on,
Punctuation's rivers, drawn,
Crafting landscapes with our prose,
Where every letter, rightly chose.

In the alchemy of alphabets and sounds,
A quiet peace is often found,
The writer's craft, a haven's tent,
Within the realm of sentiment.

Heartstrings and Hyphens

Connections formed, a line, a dash,
Stories told in a fleeting flash,
Heartstrings pull, emotions merge,
In the rhythm of life, a surging surge.

With every breath, a link is made,
In hyphen-steps, love is conveyed,
The bond that ties a tender trap,
In dashes small, a world, perhaps.

Interwoven threads, a tapestry,
Of joys and woes, a vast sea,
Pauses within our tale so spun,
By hyphens joined, we become one.

Sentences stretch across the void,
Punctuated love, not to avoid,
The tales we tell with ink and pen,
In hyphens found, again, again.

The Heart's Palette

In hues of red, our pulses dance,
A symphony within the chest,
Where love and passion take their stance,
On the heart's canvas, feelings rest.

In whispers green and envy bold,
Our human flaws in colors roll,
Yet amidst shades, compassion's gold,
Heals the canvas of the soul.

With streaks of sorrow, tints of blue,
Grief washes over, yet we strive,
For on this palette, hope's hue,
Keeps the art of heart alive.

Yellow joy, in laughter's light,
Brushes warmth on every scene,
Mending cracks with colors bright,
The heart paints life's variegated sheen.

Silent Echoes

Whispers of a shadow's breath,
Silent echoes fill the air,
Holding secrets close to death,
In the void of vacant stare.

Murmurs lost in empty halls,
Bouncing back without a sound,
What was spoken now enthralls,
In the hush, meanings abound.

Quiet cadence of the night,
In its stillness, words resonate,
Carrying the absent light,
Conveying what we contemplate.

Silent echoes, peace imparts,
Speech within the heart's confines,
Binding us when distance parts,
In quietude, the soul aligns.

Intimate Strokes

Gentle lines across the skin,
The painter's brush, soft and tender,
Intimate strokes that begin,
To sketch the love we remember.

Each caress, a vivid line,
Forms the portrait of desire,
Where touch translates into sign,
A language of silent fire.

Fingers trace an unspoken word,
On the canvas of completion,
In this art, no voice is heard,
Yet, it echoes pure affection.

Every nuance, softly drawn,
In the gallery of devotion,
Every hue of dawn's newborn,
Captured in these intimate motions.

Shade of Sentiments

Every feeling wears a shade,
Colors of the heart's parade,
Crimson anger, cool blue sad,
Every tint of good and bad.

Joy in yellows, bright and clear,
The warm tones of laughter near,
Purple mysteries of trust,
In these shades, we find we must.

Gentle pink of love's first kiss,
An emotional chromatic bliss,
Darkened grays of fear's abyss,
In this spectrum, nothing is amiss.

Green of growth, and change, and life,
Undertones of struggle and strife,
Our sentiments in colors rife,
Shaded stories, emotionally strife.

Reflections in Resin

Trapped within this glossy tomb,
Preserving life in silence's womb.
Time suspends its hurried flight,
In amber hue and hazy light.

Twilight's secrets safely sealed,
Stories in translucent field.
Nature's art forever cast,
A moment from the distant past.

Shadows dance as light shines through,
The essence of what once was true.
Echoes of the life held dear,
In resin's grip, remain clear.

Each inclusion tells its tale,
A time capsule, trapped in detail.
A reflection held in stasis,
Beauty bound, in golden spaces.

The Essence of Expression

Words spill forth like endless rain,
Cascading thoughts a painter's stain.
They shape the air, the heart, the mind,
In the dance of truth they find.

Emotions wrapped in language's fold,
Tales of the new and echoes of old.
Expression's heart beats strong and fierce,
Crafting songs that spirits pierce.

Vibrant hues on canvas speak,
In each stroke, the soul's mystique.
Language that we barely hear,
Yet feel its essence drawing near.

Metaphor and simile blend,
Meanings twist and thoughts extend.
Expression's essence, pure, profound,
In every word, life's pulse is found.

Core Calligraphy

Ink flows deep from the core of Earth,
Calligraphy of the universe's birth.
Mountains etched in history's hand,
Landscape's script in time's sand.

Rivers carve their tales so wide,
In Earth's canvas, secrets confide.
Waves of script crash to the shore,
Telling sagas of the ocean floor.

The tree rings speak in silent script,
Of years passed, and time's adrift.
Nature's hand, so skilled and deft,
Writing life's story, right to left.

Volcanoes burst with fiery line,
Penmanship of force divine.
Calligraphy in molten stone,
Earth's deep words in ash are sown.

Whispering Words

In the silence of the midnight breeze,
The trees whisper words with ease.
Leaves rustling soft and low,
Secrets only the night does know.

The stars above in quiet speech,
The dreams of the cosmos within reach.
The moon's hushed tones to Earth descend,
Her silver script the skies doth pen.

Gentle murmurs of the stream,
Crafting sonnets in the dream.
Flowing water's silent say,
Scrolling epics night and day.

Whispers woven in the air,
A symphony of voiceless prayer.
Words unspoken, yet understood,
The quiet eloquence of life's neighborhood.

Beneath the Ballpoint

Ink rolls out like a silent shout,
Across the page, a dance devout.
Beneath the grip, ideas sprout,
Tales unwind, in cursive flout.

Scribbles curve, they twist and bend,
Underneath the pressures penned.
Narratives fight to extend,
In every line, a hidden friend.

Whorls of blue upon the white,
Stories hidden from the light.
Ballpoint's journey into night,
Reveals the heart's quiet fight.

Gentle scratches, marks of thought,
Where battles of expression fought.
In inked abyss, dreams are caught,
Beneath the ballpoint, words are wrought.

Scripted Soulstice

When words align with solstice sun,
The page ignites as thoughts do run.
With pen in hand, the script has begun,
Scribing the soulstice, second to none.

Longest day meets shortest night,
Verses cast in the warmest light.
Ponderings in the sun's clear sight,
The scripted soulstice takes its flight.

Characters dance in sun's embrace,
Waltzing with such eloquent grace.
Every line a warm trace,
Of poetic touch in time's own space.

As dusk descends, ink still flows,
In the quietude, creativity grows.
Through the night, the manuscript glows,
Preserving soulstice in poetic prose.

Veiled Thoughts

Behind the veil where thoughts reside,
Silent echoes of the inner tide.
Unseen notions that there abide,
Awaiting their moment to be untied.

The quiet rumble of ideas unspoken,
Shrouded in silence, like promises broken.
Veiled thoughts, like dreams awoken,
Seek the light, their truth the token.

Words linger veiled in the shrouds of mind,
In webs of mystery, uniquely designed.
Each thread a story that's yet to find,
The path from the shadows, released, unconfined.

Once unveiled by courage's quest,
Ideas journey from the nest.
Freed from confines where they rest,
Vital thoughts, at last, expressed.

Silhouetted Sonnets

In twilight's tender sorrow softly held,
A silhouette of sonnets, love's caress,
Beneath the crescent moon's embracing arch,
Whispers of the night, in shadows dressed.

The darkened figure dances with the stars,
Each motion scribes a verse on velvet sky,
As zephyrs hum the tune of ancient scars,
The sonnet's heart in each exhale and sigh.

Yet silhouetted 'gainst the fading light,
The syllables of soul find their release,
In elegant embrace of day and night,
They pen a silent opus of peace.

And in the hush, before the dawn's soft sonnet,
Lies dreams in silhouette, the stars upon it.

Undertones Unveiled

Beneath the spoken word, a whisper lies,
A subtle undertone, truth's soft attire,
Unveiled through knowing smiles, and knowing eyes,
It sings a tune that silent lips admire.

For underneath the surface stir the depths,
Where hidden rhythms pulse with life unseen,
A canvas deep where murky mystery creeps,
In undertones of teal and sapphire sheen.

So listen to the hush of heartfelt hues,
That paint the honest shades of inner themes,
In unveiling quiet, authenticity brews,
And in between the lines, genuineness gleams.

Undertones unveiled, the soul's own speech,
The whispers beneath words, only hearts can teach.

Whims of the Will

Upon the winds of whim do fancies fly,
With willful waltz, they dance, they dare, they dart,
The heart's caprice takes wing 'neath open sky,
A merry masquerade that plays its part.

Such whims are weaved within the will's own wile,
The threads of dreams are spun before the dawn,
The tapestry of mind meets miracle's mile,
As wishes in the will's own weave are born.

The will, it whispers, 'Follow where I lead,'
'Cross fields of fervor, through the streams of stride,
For in the journey's joy is life's fine creed,
And in the gallant gusts, our souls confide.

Whims of the will, with wayward breezes blend,
In serendipitous paths that twist and wend.

Secrets in Script

In scrolls and scrawls, secrets softly sleep,
Scripted in the silence of the mind,
In inks of introspection, thoughts run deep,
Entwined in tales that trust the heart to find.

Letters lock away the lore of life,
In cryptic codes and ciphers bold and bare,
The parchment bears the burdens, joy, and strife,
A hidden history in handwriting fair.

Each stroke, a secret kept from common view,
With loops and lines, the soul's own language shown,
A memoir made for me, for you, to rue,
In scripted sigils, inner truths are known.

So in the script, the secrets are conveyed,
The quiet confessions of the heart displayed.

Disguised Descriptions

Beneath the masks of mirth and grin,
We hide our hearts, the truth within.
A masquerade of joy we wear,
Yet underneath, it's just bare air.

In laughter's cloak, we often shroud,
The inner cries that speak out loud.
But eyes, those tell-tale signs reveal,
A soul bereft, in silent kneel.

For every smile that graces lips,
A secret script of life eclips.
Disguised descriptions we compose,
In gowns of glee, the sorrow stows.

Upon the stage of life, so vast,
We act until the very last.
The final curtain call will show,
True faces from the grand tableau.

Pulse of the Pen

In the quiet of night when thoughts cascade,
The pen starts to dance in the solitary shade.
With ink as its pulse, the blank page it courts,
Crafting dreams in script, it confidently sports.

A rhythm is found in each deliberate stroke,
Bringing life to ideas, as soft words provoke.
It bleeds in patterns of blue and of black,
Transfusing emotion from the heart it packs.

A pulse that quickens with tales to tell,
Through peaks and troughs, it rises and fell.
In the symphony of silence, it finds its beat,
Engaging the soul in a feat so neat.

The pen slows, the crescendo fades to rest,
Imprinting the journey it has confessed.
The pulse may still, yet in those lines,
It whispers its legacy, through time it shines.

Labyrinth of Language

Words wind down like ancient paths,
Through labyrinths of language, our thoughts entwined.
Each syllable, a step through the math,
Of constructing meanings, uniquely designed.

We navigate the mazes, complex and wide,
Seeking the center where understanding lies.
Twisting corridors of context abide,
Where the echo of our intent softly sighs.

Ariadne's thread is the narrative spun,
Guiding us back to where we begun.
In the dance of dialect, the exit we find,
Unraveling mysteries once confined.

This vast vernacular, intricate and grand,
Holds the key to worlds unexplored, unplanned.
In conversations, we seek and we chart,
The route through the labyrinth, heart to heart.

Shaded Soliloquies

In the shadow of my quiet repose,
I whisper soliloquies no one knows.
Flickering thoughts to the rhythm of shade,
Spilling secrets in this silent serenade.

Through the hush, my heart's voice takes flight,
Casting echoes in the canopy of night.
Recounting tales in the absence of light,
Where shadows hold my confessions tight.

Words etch a dance in the dimmed glow,
A choreographed truth I alone bestow.
Shrouded sonnets, the dusk does brace,
While I articulate my heart's quiet grace.

In shaded soliloquies, truths unmask,
Baring the soul in the evening's task.
Until the sun claims the sky's grand stage,
I'll rest in the dark, my whispered page.

Essence Etched

Upon the canvas of the skies,
My essence gently brushed.
Soft hues of hopes and wistful sighs,
In twilight's glow are hushed.

In every dream, a trace of me,
A signature unseen.
A mural of my soul, set free,
Adorns the world serene.

With every dawn, a fresh design,
Life paints with tender touch.
In every stroke, a chance to shine,
My essence etched as such.

This art of being, bold yet fine,
A dance of fate and chance.
I leave my mark, a subtle sign,
In time's eternal dance.

The Heart's Hieroglyphics

Emotions scribed in chambers deep,
A script that pulses, never sleeps.
In every beat, a story hides,
The heart's own hieroglyphic tides.

Love's cryptic language, carved within,
Unveils the tales of joy and sin.
Each rhythmic throb, a coded dance,
A silent opera of romance.

Tears stain the parchment of the soul,
Where secrets written, make us whole.
Each sob - a word, each laugh - a glyph,
In heart's hieroglyphics - life's pith.

Thus, feel each pulse as precious script,
Where through the veins, our life is slipped.
In every beat, a truth's unfurled,
The heart's hieroglyphics tell our world.

Silent Sonnets

In whispered wind and rustling leaves,
A silent sonnet finds reprieve.
Unheard, it soars on zephyr's back,
An ode to moments, still, intact.

The moonlit shadows, soft imparts,
A verse carved deep within the hearts.
A serenade to night's embrace,
In silence, love's tender trace.

Eyes speak in volumes, mute yet clear,
Expressing what no words can near.
Their silent sonnets truly known,
In quiet looks, emotions shown.

For in the hush, we understand,
The silent poems of touch, of hand.
No need for speech, as hearts confess,
In silent sonnets, souls caress.

Unspoken Utterings

Between the lines of life there lays,
Unspoken utterings, silent phrase.
The truths which tongues dare not unfold,
In silent stories, yet untold.

The glances holding words at bay,
The things that hands, not lips, convey.
Expressions deep, that voice forgot,
In gestures, spoken thoughts are caught.

Though not a sound may break the air,
Communications still declare.
With every sigh, nod, and gaze,
Unspoken utterings fill our days.

In every pause, the unsaid rests,
A realm where quietude invests.
For often more is not expressed,
In unspoken utterings, hearts attest.

Vulnerable Verses

In the silence of my solitude,
I pen down my inner feud.
On paper, raw emotions bleed,
In these verses, my heart does plead.

A tapestry of hopes so frail,
Woven with a trembling gale.
Words tumble in a delicate dance,
In vulnerability, I find my chance.

Scattered thoughts like autumn leaves,
In the whirlwind of my restless heaves.
Each stanza a confession of fears,
Vulnerable Verses, a trail of tears.

Encased in rhyme, my secrets speak,
Of strength when I am truly weak.
These lines where truth converges,
Bear the weight of my purges.

Depths of My Diary

A silent guardian holds my past,
Within its pages, shadows are cast.
The depths of my diary know no end,
Every memory, every silent friend.

Beneath the cover, the whispers wait,
Of love that came too soon or too late.
Joy and sorrow in tandem stride,
In the ink, my confessions abide.

The flicker of moments, captured still,
Coaxed onto paper by sheer force of will.
Diary depths, harboring day and night,
Witness to the soul's undying fight.

Entries etched in the dead of night,
Reveal a journey outside of light.
In my diary's depths, honestly penned,
Are the tales of a heart on the mend.

Emotional Etchings

Upon the canvas of my mind,
Emotions etched, not always kind.
They carve their path with sharp intent,
In every line, my spirit's bent.

With every stroke, the truth unveiled,
On the battleground, I've often failed.
Etchings of joy, etchings of pain,
Reminders that nothing is in vain.

A chronicle of the heart's deep scars,
Underneath the ceaseless stars.
Tales of love that's born, then smothered,
Within these etchings, feelings are covered.

The artistry of a soul that bleeds,
The emotional etchings, sowing seeds.
Within the verses, find my teachings,
About love, life, and heartfelt pleadings.

Intimate Impressions

Whispers of the heart, softly tread,
On the delicate ground where feelings spread.
Intimate impressions, gently born,
On the silent canvas of the morn.

Each impression a tender touch,
Revealing the depths that matter much.
In lines of love, pain, and pleasure,
Each a private, treasured treasure.

In the solace of the night's embrace,
I trace these impressions I cannot erase.
They are the quiet sighs of the soul's confession,
Lingering long, an indelible impression.

Intimacies laid on the page in script,
Where my heart's softest whispers are dipped.
In these impressions, find my heart's caress,
In the quietude of my silent express.

Nostalgic Notations

On the canvas of the past, light strokes of memory,
Faded edges of laughter, a time-tested ceremony.
In the halls of thought, echo footsteps old,
Shadows of yesteryears, in silence, they unfold.

Pages of the heart, turned with gentle care,
Imprints of the first smile, whispers of dare.
Sunsets long forgotten, now blush once more,
The scent of the old tree, by the childhood shore.

Melodies linger on, in quiet repose,
The clink of the bike, the bloom of the rose.
Twilight brings the soft hum of home's embrace,
Nostalgic notations, time cannot erase.

Essence Excerpts

Through veils of the cosmos, a soul's silent plea,
A dance of existence, as deep as the sea.
Light cascading softly, nature's tender script,
These are the essence excerpts, quietly kept.

In a drop of morning dew, the world's reflection,
A moment of serenity in perfect introspection.
Whispers of the heart, so faint, yet so strong,
In the essence excerpts, we find where we belong.

The core of the petal, perfection's own sphere,
The essence of joy is a child's laughter clear.
Within us resides, this pure distillate,
In essence excerpts, life we contemplate.

Vivid Veins

Rivers of life on the surface of skin,
A map of our journeys, outside and within.
These vivid veins, a testament to strife,
Carry the elixir, the very flow of life.

They branch and they meander, pathways so keen,
Underneath the surface, so clear yet unseen.
The pulse of existence, in crimson and blue,
Vivid veins tell stories, each one anew.

Through valleys of flesh, secrets they weave,
The rhythm of heartbeats, in which we believe.
In these vivid veins, our essence does dwell,
The spirit's calligraphy, penned very well.

A network of vitality, a script so divine,
Vivid veins, with life's manuscript, intertwine.
The throb of adventure, the rush of the fight,
In the network of veins, courses the light.

Metaphors of the Mind

In the theater of thoughts, ideas play the lead,
Where dreams are the script, on which our hearts feed.
The stage is set with memories, in light and in shade,
Metaphors of the mind, in grand masquerade.

Silent soliloquies whisper in mental halls,
As wisdom and folly on the scenery calls.
With every emotion, a new scene is set,
In metaphors of the mind, life's puzzle we bet.

A carousel of concepts, spinning with grace,
Each horse a notion, keeping pace in the race.
The mind's eye perceives, what reality confines,
Metaphors of the mind, in brilliant designs.

In the garden of intellect, thoughts bloom like flowers,
Watered by experience, kissed by knowledge showers.
In this cerebral landscape, where insight does wind,
Grow the metaphors of the mind, forever entwined.

www.ingramcontent.com/pod-product-compliance
Lightning Source LLC
LaVergne TN
LVHW012244070526
838201LV00090B/110